I0157572

Fire of God

Cheryl Jones-Ross

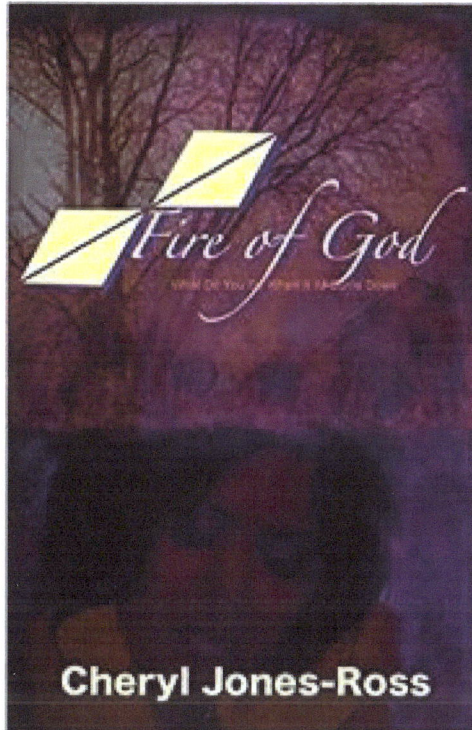

(Workbook and Study Guide)

"Fire of God" Workbook

Pastor Cheryl Jones-Ross

Scriptures marked KJV are the King James Version, Public Domain.

"Italics in Scripture quotations have been added by the author for emphasis."
Library of Congress Cataloging-in-Publication Data

Names: Cheryl Jones-Ross. Author
Fire of God
(Workbook and Study Guide)
Description:
Identifiers: LCCN 2017932357   ISBN (978-0-9986654-2-9)
Copyright © 2017 by (Cheryl Jones-Ross)
Brtyca Publishing

All rights reserved. No part of this book may be reproduced or transmitted in any form or by any means without written permission from the author.

CONTENTS

This study guide is not a replacement for professional counseling. We suggest that if you feel that you need more in-depth help in dealing with grief, that you see a qualified professional.

We also suggest that you read the entire book "Fire of God" as most questions refer to particular passages from the book.

This guide can be used in a classroom setting or it can be used individually in your private study and meditation time with the Lord.

Introduction

1. We must understand that pain is also a necessary season in our lives because:

_____

_____

_____

_____

_____

Read Jeremiah 15:18:

Jeremiah was in so much pain that he said to God wilt thou be altogether unto me as a liar, and as waters that fail? In other words have you lied to me God? Has this word that I speak about, that I live about, that I preach about failed in my own life and that is why I am suffering like this? You see pain will make you almost call God a liar, pain can cause even the most mature saint to buckle under the pressure. Have you ever seen somebody whose pain level is so high till they were almost out of their mind in pain. I have and that type of pain will test, it will prove what is really in you.

But look at what God says! God didn't say, my son, I see that you have had enough, (and there will come a time when God will say it is enough). But God told Jeremiah, if thou will take forth the precious from the vile, thou shalt be as my mouth:

If you will endure the bitterness of what you are going through, it

WILL make you better. If you will take the precious, meaning precious stones and the jewels from that pain that is being poured out in your life, stones that will be used in building you up. If you would take that from the very pain that you want to get away from because you think it is worthless, or insignificant to your life, it is unnecessary, and let it do in you what it needs to do in you, God said to Jeremiah, you will be as my mouth. In other words, you will be my mouthpiece and you can say what I say and it shall be done throughout the earth.

a. What was Jeremiah's complaint to God?

_____
_____
_____
_____
_____

b. What was God's response?

_____
_____
_____
_____
_____

c. In what ways was Jeremiah being afflicted?

_____
_____
_____
_____
_____

d. How can you identify with Jeremiah's afflictions?

_____
_____
_____
_____
_____

e. What purpose do you see in your own afflictions?

_____
_____
_____
_____
_____

2. Take a moment to write down what has been your greatest affliction to date and what affect it had on your life. Allow yourself a few minutes to be open and honest with yourself in identifying if and how it has changed you.

_____
_____
_____
_____
_____
_____

(If this workbook is being completed in a classroom setting, allow participates to share their thoughts with the group in an environment of acceptance and empathy)

Chapter One

Fire Brings In A New Season

Isaiah 43:19 , *Behold, I will do a new thing; now it shall spring forth; shall ye not know it? I will even make a way in the wilderness, and rivers in the desert (KJV).*

1. Whenever the Lord brings a new dispensation or a new season into the earth or into the life of the believer, it is usually marked by_____.

2. Anytime that He wants to usher in radical changes and carry out His plan for mankind_____.

3. We must understand that the Holy Spirit helps us to live the life of Jesus and He guides us into all truth but, the fire of God is what gives us_____for His word, for His work, and _____.

4. Read Amos 6:1 and answer the following questions:

a. What warnings has the Lord given to you specifically?

_____
_____
_____
_____
_____

b. What happens when we become satisfied in our lives?

_____

_____

_____

_____

_____

c. What have you become comfortable with that you know is a hindrance in moving you forward?

_____

_____

_____

_____

_____

5. List 4 things that you will agree to do immediately to begin the process of moving ahead in your life. (List in order of priority).

1._____

2._____

3._____

4._____

Chapter Two

Fire is Extreme

Jesus told John to *write the church at Laodecia and say, These things saith the Amen, the faithful and true witness, the beginning of the creation of God, I know thy works, that thou art neither cold nor hot: I would thou wert cold or hot. So then because thou art lukewarm, and neither cold nor hot, I will spue thee out of my mouth (KJV).*

1. In every single letter that the Lord wrote to the seven churches, He said_____.

2. Why do you think that Jesus specifically addressed "works" and not "relationship" in this scripture?

_____
_____
_____
_____
_____
_____

3. What does it mean to be "lukewarm"?

_____
_____
_____
_____

4. Do you believe that you are "lukewarm"? Why or Why not?

_____

_____

_____

_____

_____

5. Read Psalms 38:5 and answer the following questions.

    a. What was David's revelation in this scripture?

_____

_____

_____

_____

_____

    b. In what way or ways can you relate to David's summation of his life?

_____

_____

_____

_____

_____

6. What is difference between God's permissive will and His perfect will?

_____

_____

_____

_____

_____

7. Do you believe that your life's mission is totally surrendered to the Lord's perfect will for your life?_____Explain

_____

_____

_____

_____

_____

_____

_____

Take time to pray and ask the Lord to reveal to you what His plan is for your life and Read Genesis 37: 5-11. Consider some ways in which the Lord may have spoken to you concerning His plan for your life.

8. Do you believe that you are making a difference in the lives of the people that are in your sphere of influence._____Explain?

_____

_____

_____

_____

_____

_____

_____

_____

_____

9. How can you be even more impactful?

_____

_____

_____

_____

_____

10. Name some ways in which Jesus was impactful in His ministry.

_____

_____

_____

_____

_____

11. In what way or ways does our own personal ministry compare to His?

_____

_____

_____

_____

_____

Chapter Three

Smoke Doesn't Always Mean Fire

Psalms 104:1-4, *Bless the LORD, O my soul. O LORD my God, thou art very great; thou art clothed with honour and majesty. (KJV)*. It goes on to say in the 4th verse, *Who maketh his angels spirits; his ministers a flaming fire:(KJV)*.

"Smoke is an indicator that there may be a fire somewhere, but smoke is mainly an irritant. When we are blowing smoke we will think that we are walking in power and authority, or that we have some type of rank in the kingdom. When in fact, the things that we do will be irritating to the body of Christ".

1. Smoke occurs when there is incomplete combustion or not enough oxygen_____.

Incomplete combustion means there is not enough of the word of God to get rid of "US", not enough obedience to the word of God to kill off our flesh, not enough fellowship with HIM to cause us to really know who God is and receive His love. When there is incomplete combustion, not everything is burned or consumed. Therefore, we will be more carnally minded than spiritually minded, it is more about our will than His will, our way or no way, up one week, down the other. We will have more sorrow than joy, more confusion than there is peace.

The bible says that GOD will make his ministers a flaming fire a blazing, scorching burning, destructive fire. When we are a flaming fire. "WE" will be consumed by God, we will be purged, refined, all the impurities will be removed from our lives. Our entire life will be burned up to where we are no longer that person that we used to be. People will wonder what happened to us, how did we get so bold in God!

We must be full of the word of God, for it is the oxidizing agent (or our oxygen). His word is the air that we breathe, it is the breath of life. The fuel only reacts when there is oxygen. If fire is exposed to pure oxygen such as from an oxygen canister, combustion speeds up dramatically, and there may be an explosion. When we react to the rhema word of God, the way that the dry bones did in the valley, the breath of God will ignite an explosion in us that will set us on fire and cause us to come alive in Christ.

Read Ezekiel 37:1-14 and refer to the corresponding chapter in the book to answer this question.

2. Only the wind of God would be able to _____ in them to enforce orders and to ensure that they would be carried out as intended, and give them the authority_____, to _____ and to _____, and _____with various gifts.

3. Take a hard look at your life and list 4 qualities that you have that you know for certain rub people the wrong way.

a._____

b._____

c._____

d._____

4. Why do you think that these qualities are a problem for people?

_____
_____
_____
_____
_____

5. Which one of those qualities have caused you to get the most negative feedback from people? And Why?

_____
_____
_____
_____
_____

6. Now list 4 qualities that you believe that you possess that are qualities that are helpful to others.

a._____

b._____

c._____

d._____

7. Name a time that you thought that your actions were in line with the will of God and then discovered that what you were doing was

hurtful to others.

_____

_____

_____

_____

_____

8. How did it make you feel to discover how others were affected
by your works?

_____

_____

_____

_____

_____

9. What could or should you have done differently? And what do
you think the outcome would have been with a different approach
from you?

_____

_____

_____

_____

_____

_____

_____

_____

Chapter Four

The Furnace of Afflictions

1 Peter 4:12 says, *Beloved, think it not strange concerning the fiery trial which is to try you, as though some strange thing happened unto you: (KJV)*

1. Anyone that has been chosen by the Lord must first be_____.

2. How does the book "Fire of God" define affliction?

_____

_____

_____

_____

_____

3. Why are each of us tested?

_____

_____

_____

_____

_____

4. The trials that the Lord will send into each of our lives to purge us won't work for the other person because we each have

_____ and are

_____ and

_____.

5. God said, Behold, I have refined thee, but not with silver; I have chosen thee in the furnace of affliction (KJV). What does that word "chosen" mean?

_____

_____

_____

_____

_____

All of us MUST suffer in some kind of way and the bible says, if we don't suffer with Christ will not reign with Christ. But some people will never have to experience that level of acute pain in our lives that must be experienced by those who bear the name of Jesus. There are some who have been chosen to carry the gospel, some of you already know this, and others have not recognized that this is why you have been suffering the way you have. Some of you know that you have been chosen for His name sake but, have not really understood the pain that this is going to cost you.

God told Ananias concerning the Apostle Paul, Go and get him: for he is a chosen vessel unto me, to bear my name before the Gentiles, and kings, and the children of Israel: For I will shew him how great things he must suffer for my name's sake.

You see, the bible says many are called (many means all), but few are chosen. All are called according to His purpose, every single one of us have a purpose for our lives, but few are chosen to bear His name.

Does that then mean the called and the chosen are greater or lesser than the other. Absolutely not! The book of Isaiah the 54 chapter the Lord said, Sing o barren thou that didn't not bear, break forth in singing and cry aloud. In other words God is saying to the called, rejoice that you did not suffer the type of pain that one suffers who bears the word of God. Cry aloud that thou didst not travail (or writhe) with child.

Some of us will never have to go through that type of child bearing pain. And God is saying to you, rejoice, shout, and celebrate the fact that you will still be a partaker of His blessings even though you did not have to go through the type of travail that comes with bearing the gospel of Jesus Christ.

6. The Lord has prepared a furnace for all of us in order to remove the impurities from our lives. List some impurities, that may be a hindrance to anyone wanting to move forward in God.

_____

_____

_____

_____

_____

_____

_____

_____

7. In the book, the author references the testing of the three Hebrew boys in the fiery furnace. Read Daniel 3:19-25 and choose three main points that you pulled from this passage.

1.

2.

3.

8. Why did you choose these three and how do they correspond to the trials that are or happening or have happened in your life?

_____

_____

_____

_____

_____

Chapter Five

This is My Fire

Daniel 33:22 Therefore because the king's commandment was urgent, and the furnace exceeding hot, the flame of the fire slew those men that took up Shadrach, Meshach, and Abednego.

1. Chapter 4 concludes by saying, "Remember, the men that threw the three Hebrew boys in the fiery furnace? They died at the door of the furnace because that fire was not their fire." What was the message that the author was trying to send through that statement?

_____
_____
_____
_____
_____

2. The above scriptures says that the King gave an urgent commandment to throw the Hebrew boys in the fire. Have you every felt as if though a trial that you were thrust into came upon you with an urgency?_____
Explain_____

_____
_____
_____

3. What was your initial reaction to the onset of that trial?

_____

_____

_____

_____

_____

4. How does your initial reaction compare to your response to the end of that same trial?

_____

_____

_____

_____

_____

5. The King commanded that they should heat the furnace one seven times more than it was "wont" to be heated. Why did he make such a request?

_____

_____

_____

_____

_____

6. Name a time in your life when you felt disgraced or humiliated by a particular trial in your life.

_____

_____

_____

_____

_____

7.What was your response or reaction with regard to how you felt?

_____

_____

_____

_____

_____

8. Did you blame someone else for feeling humiliated and if so was that blame justified?_____ Why or why not?

_____

_____

_____

_____

_____

9. Do you believe that you are still holding on to that blame? Yes or No_____Explain your answer.

_____

_____

_____

_____

_____

Read Numbers 31:22

10. What does this scripture mean?

_____

_____

_____

_____

_____

11. Name some qualities that you possess that are valuable to God?

_____

_____

_____

_____

_____

_____

12. Explain why they may be of value and how can you maximize on those qualities?

_____

_____

_____

_____

_____

Chapter Six

Trial By Fire

1 Chronicles 4:9 And Jabez was more honourable than his brethren: and his mother called his name Jabez, saying, Because I bare him with sorrow.

Read 1 Chronicles 4:9-10

1. What does the name Jabez mean and how did he get that name?

_____
_____

2. Name three reasons why the Lord would call Jabez "honorable"?
     1._____
     2. _____
     3. _____

3. Do you believe that you are honoring the Lord through your sufferings?_____
Explain_____

_____
_____
_____
_____

Whenever we are suffering, we want God to get rid of it, or get us through it, because we just want to be done with it. But we rarely *ask the Lord to do in us what He needs to do SO THAT WE <u>CAN</u> BE DONE WITH IT.*

Many of us are still in trails because we haven't asked God WHY. If we ask why, then He can tell us what He is trying to accomplish in us so that we can yield to Him and let that pain accomplish its purpose in our lives.

Take time out to read the following study on the three things that Jabez asked the Lord for in prayer. Take a few minutes after each point to pray according to the words of Jabez and answer the questions.

1. That thine hand might be with me; *Jabez had enough wisdom, fear and humility to tell God have your way in my life, even in this.*

a. What is your "this"?

_____

_____

_____

_____

2. Keep me from evil; *While you are doing this, keep me from evil. Keep me from being miserable in this pain, keep me from being in distress, keep me from being hurt. Meaning, keep this situation, these folks, this drama, this sorrow this devastation from permanently effecting me in an adverse way so that I don't abort the process. Get everything out of me that will hinder YOUR will from being done in my life, so that I can finally say it is no longer I, but Christ that lives in me and the life that I now live, I live it by the faith of the son of God who loved me and gave himself for me. Don't let what you are doing be disagreeable to me. I am not asking to escape the pain (even though I sure want to), but help me to agree*

with its purpose and <u>endure it.</u>

    a. Is there anything that the Lord has allowed to happen in your life that you have not come into agreement with?_____If your answer is Yes, Write down why you believe that you are struggling to agree with what the Lord has allowed to happen in your life.

_____

_____

_____

_____

_____

_____

    3. And enlarge my coast; *All of us have something on the inside of us that the Lord wants to enlarge, that he wants to broaden to expand in the earth because your gifts, your talents, your callings are not simply just for you to enjoy. God didn't give you those talents, those abilities that treasure for you to do whatever YOU want to do with it. But God has placed that treasure in you so that you can occupy, do kingdom business, expand, increase, take over the world. But, you must be willing to humble yourselves and allow HIM to do what He needs to do in you in order to get rid of the impurities, the sin, the "I" mentality, everything in your life that will not give HIM glory through your gifts and your purpose.*

    a. Name three things that you are asking the Lord to do in your life and commit to praying over these three things for the next 4 weeks.

1._____

2._____

3._____

Heavenly Father, I pray that the eyes and the hearts of your servants be opened to seeing and doing your will. I pray that you will help them to endure sufferings and overcome the temptation to abort the process. I pray that you will give them the desires of their heart as they yield every area of their lives over to you in Jesus Name.

Chapter Seven

The Residue

The worst situation of your life will be the one that will solve many of your problems and remove the stumbling blocks out of your life and bring what The Lord has said to you to conclusion.

However, you must get through the situation and deal with what you have left which is "The Residue".

The dictionary defines residue as something that remains after a part is removed, disposed of, or used. Often we come out of situations and what we are left with is instability. What we have gone through has made us emotionally and mentally unbalanced especially if we did not allow the Lord to really deal with us in it. Many of us want the Lord to deal with the situation, but won't let him deal with us in it. We want to rush through the situation when the Lord is saying, this is going to take some time. Therefore we are unstable meaning we can't be held secure in position and because we are unstable we really can not effectively minister to the people.

1. Name a time in your life when you were going through something that shook your spiritual foundation.

_____

_____

_____

_____

_____

2. How did that particular situation end?

_____

_____

_____

_____

_____

3. Do you feel that the outcome had a negative or positive affect on you?

_____

Explain:

_____

_____

_____

_____

_____

4. How did your attitude change after the situation had ended?

_____

_____

_____

_____

_____

Psalms 48:2-3 *Beautiful for situation, the joy of the whole earth, is mount Zion, on the sides of the north, the city of the great King.*

Zion was beautiful because of its position, its height, its elevation. Often we are impressed by the elevation of a person, however Zion was not beautiful because of its position or because of its elevation. It was beautiful because of HOW it got to its position.

5. Write a brief description of how you overcame the most difficult

obstacle in your life.

_____

_____

_____

_____

_____

Most of are happy when you have overcome. But it is not just about the fact that you overcame, But, HOW did you overcome? HOW did you get here? Did they manipulate the situation? Did you do what YOU wanted to do, did you step over people and mistreat people on the way out? Because How you got here, will determine what you DO here AND it may even determine if YOU get to stay here.

Ask the Lord to help you to discover if you are stable in your actions and in your ministry or even your life. Ask Him to show you the areas in your life where you are still suffering from the residue of your past and help you to discover the necessary steps that you must take that will cause you to have some balance in your life.

Chapter Eight

Why Does This Fire Hurt

In this chapter the author speaks candidly and extensively about her relationship with her mother and the regrets that she had because that relationship was so strained. Read the entire eighth chapter and answer the following questions.

1. Is there one person in your life in which you would like to have a better relationship with? Yes or No_____

Explain your answer.

_____
_____
_____
_____
_____

2. Is there one person in your life who would like to have a better relationship with you, but you have not forgiven that person for past hurts or disagreements? Yes or No_____

Explain your answer.

_____
_____
_____
_____
_____

3. When dealing with people, are you quicker to cast blame or accept responsibility for relationship issues. Answer and explain your answer.

_____

_____

_____

_____

_____

_____

I will forever regret the fact that I had a strained relationship with my mom. I wish that I had been a better daughter and that I could have really gotten a chance to know her as a person instead of as the mother that I thought she was. I see so much of my mother in me and in my own daughter, with whom I have been blessed to have an amazing relationship with. I will never know what my life would have been like if my mother would have lived through the tumultuous times of my early adulthood. Would I have ever gotten it together or would my turbulent relationship with her pushed me further away from listening to her advice? Would she be proud of who I am now, would my children have loved her, would she be a doting grandmother? Would we have the type of relationship that I yearn to be able to have with her as a grown woman with children and grandchildren of my own?

4. Name a time that you took the first step to reconcile with someone that you were at odds with and what was that person's response.

_____

_____

_____

_____

_____

5. How did their response make you feel?

_____

_____

_____

_____

_____

6. If you had one "do-over" in handling an adverse situation with someone in your life, write about that situation and how you would have handled it differently so that your response would be pleasing to God.

_____

_____

_____

_____

_____

_____

_____

_____

_____

_____

_____

Chapter Nine

Out of The Ashes

We often pray and beg the Lord to get us out of certain situations. I did this for the entire eight years that I was in that abusive marriage. But I didn't ask the Lord to fix me in that situation. We invite the Lord into our mess in the way that my sister did on that bathroom floor, but we don't often invite him to do away with the stench of it and to clean up the mess that is on the inside of us. Therefore, we overcome those situations but, we are covered in ashes throughout each new season in our life.

Read Psalms 50:2

1. What was the first thing that the Lord told Zion to do?

_____

_____

_____

_____

2. Name at least one thing in your life that you are still dealing with from your past. (Be honest with yourself).

_____

_____

_____

_____

_____

_____

3. Describe how it has affected your ability to be affective in the things that you have purposed in your heart to do.

_____

_____

_____

_____

_____

Isaiah 52:2 says, Shake thyself from the dust; arise, and sit down, O Jerusalem: loose thyself from the bands of thy neck, O captive daughter of Zion…

God was saying to Zion before you can arise, before you can come on the scene on my behalf and represent me, you have got to shake off the ashes, the debris, the mortar, the ore. Shake off the flesh, shake off the world, shake off that human nature, that carnal mind. Get rid of all of those ashes.

4. Explain what the Lord was saying to Zion in this scripture and what it means in your life in particular.

_____

_____

_____

_____

_____

_____

_____

Ashes are a representation of the flesh and our flesh must be dealt with. Therefore. we must first have ben proven or tested in obscurity, in those places and things that seem unimportant. If you have not been tried in insignificance, meaning you must be tried when you have the quality of being too small or unimportant to be worth consideration in order to get rid of your flesh, then you have no right to operate in the things of God.

5. Have you ever felt insignificant in your family, on your job or in ministry and what were your emotions during those times.

_____

_____

_____

_____

_____

_____

6. What have you learned for those experiences?

_____

_____

_____

_____

_____

_____

Chapter Ten

What Do You Do When It All Burns Down

I was at the end of myself.

There were many times in this process that I found myself asking the Lord, "What is wrong with me? Why can't I just be me". I had come to understand that "Me," was often very hard for people to handle because I had zeal but no knowledge of what the Lord really desired. But I continue to push people, to push situations, and that drive that I had began to drive people away because there was way too much of "me" involved. To say that "I" could be a bit "much" is an understatement and yet I knew that there had to be a need for something that was in me or else the Lord would not have made me that way.

There comes a time in our lives when we have to face the grim fact that we are imperfect and that our imperfections have caused major issues in our lives.

1. Have people refused to deal with you because of your imperfections?
Explain_____

_____

_____

_____

_____

2. Do you feel as if though you are the cause of being held back from moving ahead in ministry, business or your personal life? Is so why and if not why?

_____
_____
_____
_____
_____

"The Lord wanted me to understand that those qualities in me were valuable, but He needed to take control of me so that He could use those attributes for His own purpose."

3. When the Lord looks at you, what do you think that He sees?

_____
_____
_____
_____
_____

4. List 5 scriptures in which the Lord speaks about "you" in a favorable way.

     a. _____
     b._____
     c._____
     d._____
     e._____

5. What do you see when you look inside of yourself?

_____
_____
_____
_____

6. If question 3 and 4 do not come into agreement, what do you believe needs to transpire in your life so that you can see yourself the way the Lord sees you.

_____

_____

_____

_____

_____

7. Name a time that you heard the voice of the Lord telling you to fix some imperfection in your life and you disobeyed.

_____

_____

_____

_____

_____

8. What were the consequences of your actions?

_____

_____

_____

_____

_____

_____

9. In what way or ways did the Lord speak to you?

_____

_____

_____

_____

_____

10. Do you believe that you have a clear understanding that it was Him that was speaking?_____ Why or Why not?

_____

_____

_____

_____

_____

11. The author speaks of coming to the end of herself. What do you think that she meant?

_____

_____

_____

_____

_____

12. How can you identify with that statement?

_____

_____

_____

_____

_____

Chapter Eleven

Fire Brings Zeal

2 Corinthians 9:2. For I know the forwardness of your mind, for which I boast of you to them of Macedonia, that Achaia was ready a year ago; and your zeal hath provoked very many (KJV).

1. Name some changes in life that the author experienced after the death of her beloved sister.

_____

_____

_____

_____

_____

_____

_____

Pray and ask for discernment regarding anything that you may be refusing to let go of in order to release God's fire in your life.

Action Plan for releasing the Fire of God in your own life

1. Recognize That You Have a Problem.

   If you continue to believe that you are perfect and that there is nothing wrong with you even when others can clearly see it, you have problem. Ask God to show you any character flaws that are affecting your ability to be all that He has created you to be.

2. Recognize That You Are the Problem.

Look in the mirror. Not just the mirror on the wall, but the mirror that is on the inside of you clearly telling you that you are the problem. If everyone that you encounter says the same thing about you, then you must understand that they are not all wrong. You may very well be the problem. When you discover that you are at fault, forgive yourself and make the necessary corrections in your life.

3. Deal With Your Past.

If you fail to deal with your past you will always take the past with you. Forget those things which are behind. Forgetting doesn't mean not remembering even though we should make an effort to forget but, it means that you are no longer affected by your past. Stop letting the past dictate your present. Yes, it happened but, it is a part of the "all things" that have worked together for your good. Face up to past mistakes and then disconnect yourself from its hold on your life.

4. Deal With You.

Don't wait for the Lord to deal with you, beat Him to it. If you don't, you will experience the chastening of the Lord. Even though God's chastening is for our profit, it is not necessary that we get to that point in our lives where we must be "spanked' for our behavior or wrongdoings.

- Be quick to reconcile relationships.
- Get a hold of your emotions and thoughts.
- Be the first to do the word.
- Be the last to have a bad attitude.

5. Come to terms with your past.

There is a real difference in dealing with your past and in coming to terms with your past. When you deal with your past, your past no longer affects you, but when you come to terms with your past, your past will be your best instructor and your closes associate. Use your past as the springboard for your future and allow even the most traumatic situations to push you into God's plan and purpose for your life. Use your past as a teaching tool for others and as a testimony for the Glory of God. Remember, your past is your future!

6. Forgive.

If you don't forgive, God will not forgive you. Forgiveness releases you from people, places and things. The greatest power that a person can have over you is unforgiveness. Most likely, you are the only one who is still angry. That person may have moved on and has forgiven you, but your mind is so filled with thoughts about that person until bitterness is taking root on the inside of you. It is that bitterness that is causing your health to decline and causing you to be mean and angry and hard to work with. That person may very well want to reconcile with you but is afraid to because they know that you are the one who is holding the grudge and refusing to forgive them. Let it go, forgive and be free to live!

7. Live!

Yes, Live! You must know that is alright to be happy. It is okay to be prosperous and be successful. As a matter of fact that is the Lord's will for us that we prosper and be in health even as our souls prosper. Your happiness and success will cost you something but know that the cost will never be more than the blessings that are in store for your life. Make it your priority to live every single day and find ways to make YOU happy, but not at the expense of others. Laugh and be merry and live life to the fullest.

8. Go Forth With Fire And Zeal.

Lastly, move ahead with excitement and passion. Your passion will be ignited once you have allowed the Lord to remove any perfections in your life that are limiting you. Allow that zeal to move you forward in the will of God. It will burn the pathway to your success and keep your heart and mind through Christ Jesus in accordance to God's plan for your life.

www.ingramcontent.com/pod-product-compliance
Lightning Source LLC
Chambersburg PA
CBHW042114040426
42448CB00003B/268